PREFACE

As with all of my other books, <u>A Creative Approach To Practicing Jazz</u> is a response to my own needs and those of my colleagues and students. When, where, what and how to practice are questions that confront all serious musicians from the beginning to the end of their careers. This book represents a modest effort at addressing some of these concerns. It is not intended to replace strategies, techniques, and practice routines that have proven successful to the individual performer but rather to energize the act of practicing by offering alternatives and imaginative, often unusual, routes to the goal of excellence.

The materials contained in <u>A Creative Approach To Practicing Jazz</u> are the result of more than 45 years of trial and error, experimentation, and observing and analyzing the practice habits and attendant successes of the world's most accomplished musicians, resulting in the formulation and refinement of various techniques and strategies for deriving maximum benefits from the time spent in the practice room. While many of the routines in this book are applicable, and indeed beneficial, to the practicing of any kind of music, the main purpose, objective, and thrust is the development and enhancement of skills particular to the jazz idiom.

Some of the strategies suggested are simply highly focused and sophisticated variants of practice habits already in place for many musicians; others represent the codification of such informal approaches as playing with actual recordings (not play-a-longs) or practicing performing. All of the exercises involve the imposition of constraints designed to sharpen focus and intensify the powers of concentration.

If approached with an open mind, a healthy work ethic, a willingness to invest quality time, and the courage to be forced out of an all-too-familiar comfort zone mentality, <u>A Creative Approach To Practicing Jazz</u> will provide the challenge and modus operandi to take your playing to new and exhilarating heights.

David Baker
Summer 1994

TABLE OF CONTENTS

I. General Suggestions for Constructive Practice 1

II. Imaginative Scale Practicing 4

III. Imposing Melodic, Harmonic, and Dynamic Constraints 15

IV. Strategies Imposing Rhythmic Constraints (Plus) 17

V. A Strategy for Practicing Formulae 23

VI. A Practice Technique for Internalizing the Sound of Changes 27

VII. Practicing Changes on "Three Levels" 31

VIII. The "Twice-As-Long" Song 34

IX. Tune Learning Strategies 36

X. A Practice Technique For Using Bebop Tunes as a Tool for Learning and Internalizing the Bebop Language 39

XI. Transcribing as a Practice (Study) Technique 44

XII. Practicing With Play-A-Longs 47

XIII. How To Practice with Actual Recordings 49

XIV. "The Game" 50

XV. Practicing Performing 54

XVI. Practicing Reading Skills Using Transcribed Solos 56

XVII. Improving Your Reading Using Fakebooks 57

XVIII. Evaluating Your Playing 58

APPENDIX A: A List of Essential Bebop Tunes for Memorization 59

APPENDIX B: Bibliography 62

Published by
JAMEY AEBERSOLD JAZZ®
P.O. Box 1244
New Albany, IN 47151-1244
www.jazzbooks.com
ISBN 978-1-56224-033-2

Cover Design
JASON A. LINDSEY

CHAPTER I

General Suggestions for Constructive Practice

1. Determine the amount of time that you can realistically spend in practice.

2. When possible, spread the practice sessions out across the day.

3. Practice every day, preferably at the same time(s).

4. Articulate your goals and purposes, both general and specific as well as long-range and short-range.

5. Your practice sessions should include:

    a   maintenance (warm-ups, flexibility exercises, articulation and range exercises, and other daily routines)

    b. scales and arpeggios

    c. formulae such as II V7 patterns, cycles, turnarounds, melodic-rhythmic and harmonic patterns (clichés), bebop and contemporary patterns, etc.

    d. solo transcription (written and aural)

    e. listening

    f. ear training

    g. sight-reading changes

    h. preparing specific assignments (if you are studying)

    i. learning tunes (include all types -- blues, ballads, bebop, standards, Latin, free, contemporary, etc.)

    j. whatever else is relevant to you musically

    When practicing the above materials, vary all of the components -- tempo, dynamics, rhythm, meter, articulation, phrasing, octave placement, vibrato, inflection, mood, style, etc. Don't spend all of your practice time on things that you can already do. When the things on which you're working become comfortable, then something has to change if growth is to continue. Play the material faster, cleaner, louder, softer, higher, lower, in a different key, or with alterations; or simply add new material).

6. Develop the habit of singing your ideas before you play them. Sing along with your playing if your instrument does not involve blowing. If you play a wind instrument, "sing" in your mind.

7. Use a metronome as one means of measuring growth.

8. Play chord changes and tunes on a keyboard instrument.

9. Learn all music by rote whenever possible.

10. Never allow yourself the luxury of complacency or self-satisfaction.

11. Always try to bring something of yourself to every musical situation.

12. From time to time, tape your practice sessions and listen to them critically.

13. Work for total concentration.

14. Work for consistency.

15. Some time every day should be spent in mental practice away from the instrument. When practicing in this manner, imagine all of the mental and muscular actions of an actual performance. A decided advantage to mental practicing is that it can be done anywhere and at any time.

16. Maintaining a proper attitude and a good mood can have an excellent effect on your practicing.

17. Where you practice can seriously affect the quality of your practice. The room should be well-ventilated, well-lighted, and free of distracting elements such as extraneous noise.

18. Keep the materials handy that you will need in a practice session, such as pencils, manuscript paper, an adjustable music stand, a large mirror (if you play a wind or string instrument or sing), a metronome, extra reeds, valve or slide oil, extra strings, rosin, etc.

19. Practice meticulously and with discipline.

20. Don't practice when you are fatigued. You will usually end up doing more harm than good.

21. Keep some challenge in your practice routine. If there is no challenge, change your routine. Try to keep your goal just beyond your reach. Once a goal is achieved, move on!

22. From time to time, clean out your practice baggage. Many times you will find that what you are practicing is no longer relevant and that the problem the routine was designed to address has been solved, or that the routine is simply a habit with no particular use. The relevant question is "Why am I practicing this routine?"

23. From time to time, read tunes and changes from a fakebook. Simply play through them for familiarity; don't work on them.

24. From time to time, sing and tape solos on tunes and transcribe them. You will often be surprised at the quality of the ideas that you sing. It will do wonders for your confidence.

25. Work on the tune that you didn't know or that gave you trouble on last night's gig.

26. Work on or learn the piece that caught your fancy on the radio, T.V., movie, elevator muzak, in the club you went to, etc. Don't procrastinate. Learn it now!

27. Be critical of your playing.

28. Be your own teacher. Keep a checklist for measuring your own growth.

29. Remember: Practice doesn't make perfect, perfect practice makes perfect. Those who fail to prepare, prepare to fail.

CHAPTER II

Imaginative Scale Practicing

Practice all genre scales in the following ways:

- starting on the lowest note playable on your instrument and going to the highest comfortable note

- ascending and descending

- in all keys

- at all tempos

- at all dynamic levels

- with varied articulations

- with varied colorations, that is, with variations in timbre and by using with sound-altering devices such as mutes, etc.

- varying the rhythms

All of the examples in this chapter start on either the note C or the note C# and are written as though C is the lowest note on your instrument. Please adapt these exercises to the actual range of your instrument.

Examples 1a through 1f are exercises on the major scale. In example 1a, play all 12 major scales from the lowest note on your instrument to the highest. Examples 1b through 1f are other exercises on the major scale; play these in all 12 major keys.

6

Example 2: Ascending melodic minor scales

Example 3: Whole tone scales

Example 4: Diminished scales

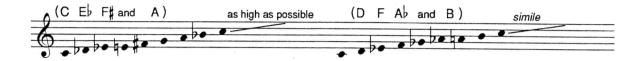

Example 5: Major pentatonic scales (in inversion the minor pentatonic)

Example 6: Blues scales

Example 7: Major scales enclosed in an octave

starting on C

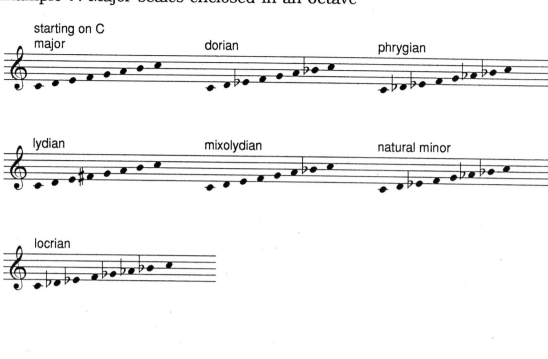

starting on Db or C#

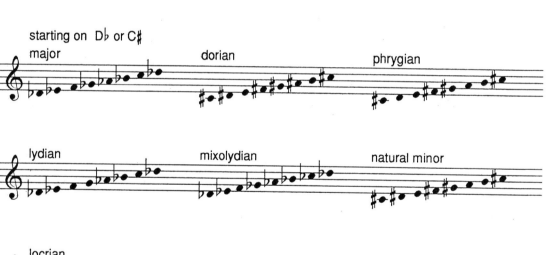

Example 8: Ascending melodic minor scales enclosed in an octave

Next, practice arbitrarily altering a note in various traditional scales, e.g., the major scale (examples 9a through 9d); the dorian scale (examples 10a through 10d); and the ascending melodic minor scale (11a through 11c). Also practice altering a note in all the different genre scales, e.g., the harmonic minor scale, the whole tone scale, the diminished scale, etc.

Once you are comfortable with altering a single tone, try altering two notes (examples 12a through 12d). Then try altering three notes (examples 13a and 13b).

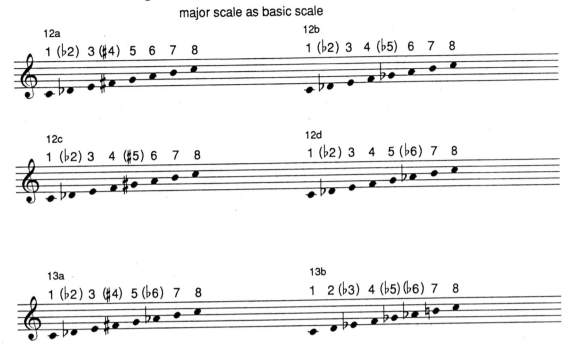

Again, once you have reached some comfort level with the aforementioned techniques, practice the various altered scales in traditional ways, e.g., broken 3rds, (examples 14a and 14b), 4ths, 5ths, 6ths, 7ths, and compound intervals such as 9ths, 10ths, etc.

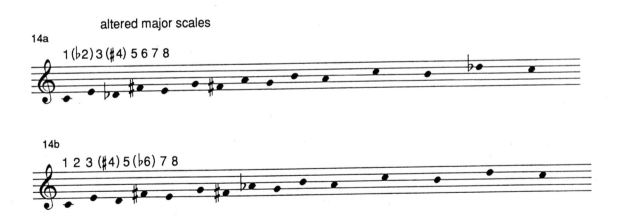

13

Also practice diatonic triads (examples 15a and 15b).

Using your imagination, extant method books, etc., devise other exercise with altered scale tones. Practice as many combinations as you can think of.

NOTE: Sing all scale exercises before attempting to play them, <u>particularly</u> those with altered tones!!

CHAPTER III

Imposing Melodic, Harmonic, and Dynamic Constraints

The following exercises are designed to improve your improvisational skills by imposing melodic, harmonic, and dynamic constraints.

1. Enclose the improvisation within an octave range. Vary the octave on subsequent choruses.

2. Improvise using only the chromatic notes of a perfect fifth, e.g., C to G.

3. Use only descending phrases.

4. Use only ascending phrases.

5. Alternate ascending and descending phrases. Also use variations such as two up and one down, two down and two up, and others.

6. Try other contrasting approaches, e.g., the following:

   a. short phrases versus long phrases
   b. high phrases versus low phrases
   c. conjunct phrases versus disjunct phrases
   d. loud versus soft
   e. consonant versus dissonant
   f. slow versus fast
   g. staccato versus legato

7. Limit the improvisation to a single rhythmic figure, two rhythmic figures, etc.

8. Start every phrase from the same note.

9. Start subsequent phrases a half-step higher than the previous one, a whole step higher, a minor third higher, etc.

10. Use only conjunct motion between phrases.

11. Start the new phrase on the last note of the previous phrase.

12. Limit the improvisation to a single scale type, e.g., whole tone, diminished, major, pentatonic, etc.

13. Limit yourself to a single defining pattern for each quality chord. (see generic patterns in chapter VI, page 27)

14. Use only the patterns from the tune itself. This approach is particularly effective on bebop tunes.

   a. Rotate the patterns.
   b. Mix the patterns.

15. Use melodic and formulaic materials from other bebop tunes.

16. Mix the tune material with fixed scales or other materials.

17. Alternate the tune materials with original improvisations.

18. Alternate phrases from two different tunes, e.g.,
     "Half Nelson"/"Groovin' High"/"Half Nelson."

19. Try playing a tune in all keys in the following manner:

     •head in the key of C
     •one chorus of improvisation in the key of C
     •head in the key of Db
     •one chorus of improvisation in the key of Db
     •etc.

20. Follow a single quote through the changes to a tune. For example,
     play a quote from "Cocktails for Two" or "Moose the Mooch" on the
     changes to "Half Nelson."

CHAPTER IV

Strategies Imposing Rhythmic Constraints (Plus)

The following exercises are designed to increase and develop rhythmic awareness; encourage and develop rhythmic independence; foster the ability to think, hear and function on several rhythmic levels simultaneously; and expand the rhythmic vision. Bebop and other jazz tunes provide a basis for practicing melodic material that will ultimately be a point of departure for improvisations.

While the primary goal of these exercises is a rhythmic one, the player is encouraged to experiment with the manipulation of other musical parameters in combination with those which are fixed either by design or choice, e.g., the following:

- changes/harmonic progression (fixed, given)
- imposed rhythm (fixed by choice)
- scale choices; scale patterns such as thirds, fourths, triads, or sevenths; diatonic versus broken motion
- range/tessitura
- dynamics
- articulations

Don't be discouraged if you are not able to do at first all that is suggested. Patience, perseverance and tenacity will ultimately get the job done.

Implementing the Strategy

1. Pick a bebop tune - e.g., "Moose the Mooche" - and play through the melodic rhythm of the entire piece using a single tone.

2. Repeat this exercise using two notes (example A), three notes (example B), or more notes (example C).

Using this approach, play a wide variety of other bebop and rhythmically interesting and challenging tunes until you have reached some level of comfort. Some suggested tunes: "Relaxin' at Camarillo," "Donna Lee," "Hot House," and "Confirmation." (see Appendix A, page 59)

3. Next try this approach using a complete scale contained within an octave. (Example A uses the major scale, example B the whole tone scale, and example C the diminished scale.)

4.   Then practice the exercise using a complete scale but without the restriction of an octave.

5.   Now try this exercise using fixed intervals (example A uses thirds, example B uses fourths) or with random movement within a given scale (example C). The fixed elements are the scale choice and the rhythm.

19

6. The next step in this approach is to begin improvising on the changes to a tune using the rhythm of the melody exclusively. You might choose to fix other parameters as well. Example A uses the following:
    •changes to "Half Nelson"
    •melodic rhythm to "Half Nelson"
    •appropriate major scales and their derivatives
    •diatonic motion exclusively
    •octave enclosed C to C

Or example B, which uses the following:
    •changes to "Half Nelson"
    •melodic rhythm to "Half Nelson"
    •appropriate major scales on I chords and the appropriate diminished scales on the II V7 groups
    •predominantly broken third movement

Or example C, which uses the following:
- •changes to "Half Nelson"
- •melodic rhythm to "Half Nelson"
- •randomly chosen appropriate scales
- •free movement within the scales

Or example D, which uses the following:
- •changes to "Half Nelson"
- •melodic rhythm to a different tune ("Groovin' High")
- •randomly chosen appropriate scales
- •free movement within the scales

From this point on, using the preceding exercises as models, devise your own routines imposing whatever constraints that will challenge you, as in the following examples:

(1)   •changes to "Confirmation"
      •melodic rhythm to "Hot House"
      •bebop scales on major chords, diminished scale on II V7s
      •enclosed octave G to G or C to C or Ab to Ab, etc.

(2)   •changes to "Donna Lee"
      •melodic rhythm to "Little Willie Leaps"
      •free scale choices
      •entire range of the instrument
      •dynamics alternating between two measures ff, two measures pp
      •two measures staccato, two measures legato

Experiment with changing any or all of the components except the given changes from chorus to chorus, as shown in the following chart:

CHORUS I	CHORUS II
a. Changes - "Groovin High"	a. "Groovin' High"
b. Melodic rhythm - "Hot House"	b. Melodic rhythm - "Joy Spring"
c. Major and whole tone scale	c. Lydian and Lydian dominant scale
d. Octave enclosed C to C	d. Two octaves enclosed G to G
e. Legato lines	e. Varied articulation
f. ppp dynamics	f. Varied dynamics

Practice these exercises with play-a-long recordings of your own choosing. Also practice them with actual recordings where you supply a rhythm counterpoint to the solo on the record.

As you can see, the possibilities for practicing along these lines are virtually limitless. The only boundaries are those of your own imagination.

CHAPTER V

A Strategy for Practicing Formulae

Although there are an infinite number of ways of combining different quality chords, there are relatively few combinations in widespread use. These combinations are called "formulae." The kinds of formulae enjoying longevity are directly related to style, era, type of tune, tempo, and many other factors.

Just as we have been able to deduce certain seemingly logical chord movements in non-jazz music -- e.g., V7 usually resolving to I or VI, IV usually going to II or V, etc. -- we can, through analysis of standards, jazz tunes, etc., extract certain formulae that greatly aid the aspiring player. Very often changes of entire sections of a tune are inter-changeable. The serious player is well-advised to seek out these building blocks and learn them in all keys and in all tempos.

One frequently-used formula:

‖   C | C | D7 | D7 | D- | G7 | C | C   ‖

Tunes which use this formula:

1. "Take the 'A' Train"
2. "The Girl From Ipanema"
3. "Mood Indigo"
4. "Solitude"
5. "Bernie's Tune" (minor)
6. "I Got It Bad"
7. "Desafinado"
8. "Those Lazy, Hazy, Crazy Days of Summer"
9. "Darktown Strutter's Ball"
10. "I Cried For You"
11. "Jersey Bounce"
12. "Crazy Rhythm"
13. "Exactly Like You"
14. "Watch What Happens"
15. "September in the Rain"
16. "I Ain't Got Nobody"
17. "These Are the Things I Love"
18. "On the Alamo"
19. "Sunny" (Jerome Kern)

How to practice this and other formulae

1. Sing/play roots.

2. Sing/play resolving sevenths. On major chords play 7 to 6, on minor chords b7 to 6, and on dominant 7th chords 4 to 3.

3. Sing/play generic pattern #1. (see chapter VI, page 27)

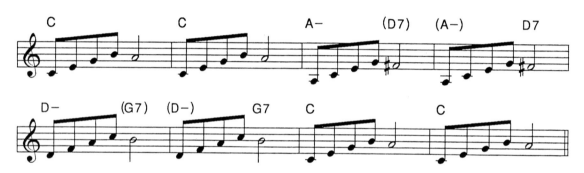

4. Sing/play generic pattern #2. (see chapter VI, page 27)

5. Sing/play the other generic patterns as outlined in chapter VI.

6. Sing/play your favorite patterns through the changes.

7. Sing/play patterns from the 55 bebop tunes. (see Appendix A, page 59)

8.   Sing/play two-octave scales through the changes.

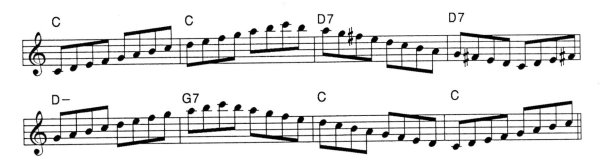

9.   Sing/play various altered chord/scales in melodic form.

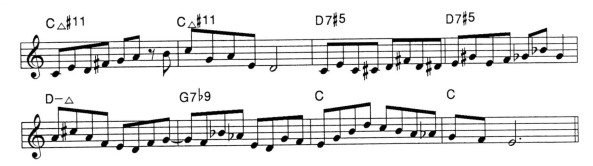

10.   Practice various substitutions for this progression.

Learn as many of the tunes based on this formula as you can.

- Practice formulae in various keys, tempos, and styles (swing, Latin, rock, fusion, ballad, etc.).

- Memorize and internalize the changes.

- Create a treasure trove of melodies based on the most frequently-used formulae. They will serve as a storehouse of raw material to be used creatively.

•Write ten new melodies in various styles and tempos on each of the major formulae. Then memorize and use them when appropriate.

•On particularly difficult changes that don't fit into traditional formulae -- "Giant Steps," "Stablemates," etc. -- write a supply of original melodies to ultimately be cannibalized.

These exercises are excellent for learning to internalize the sound of the changes of particular formulae. For a list of other important formulae see chapter 7: "Other Important Formulae in Bebop" in How to Play Bebop, vol. 2 by David Baker.

CHAPTER VI

A Practice Technique for Internalizing the Sound of Changes

The exercises in this chapter are designed to help the player articulate the basic changes to a given chord-oriented composition. I strongly suggest that the player sing these exercises through each new tune until it is completely comfortable to do so without the use of an accompanying chord-producing instrument. Then and only then should the player proceed to playing them on his/her instrument.

In these basic exercises the V chord is treated as the companion II chord (Bb7 = F-). In addition, it is possible to treat the half-diminished chord as a II; F half-diminished, for example, would be treated as F minor.

Level I Exercise: Resolving tones. For a major chord (I), move from 7 to 6 of the chord. For a minor 7th chord (II), move from the b7 to the 6 of the chord. For a dominant chord (V), move from 4 to 3 of the chord.

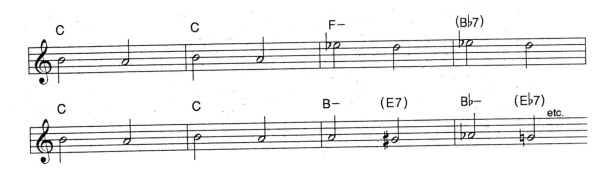

Resolving tones can also be practiced in this manner. On a major chord, move in quarter notes from the 9 to the 7 in half-steps. On a minor 7th chord, move in quarter notes from the tonic to the 6 by half-steps. On a dominant chord, move in quarter notes from the 5 to the 3 by half-steps.

Level 2 Exercise: Generic Pattern #1 (example A) and inversions (examples B and C)

Level 3 and Level 4 Exercise: Level 3 is Generic Pattern #2, and Level 4 is a double-time version of Generic Pattern #2 that allows the player to play a II-V sequence that takes place in one measure.

Level 5 Exercise: Double-time pattern for use over a chord lasting two measures. (Use Level 4 exercise for II-V sequences lasting one measure.)

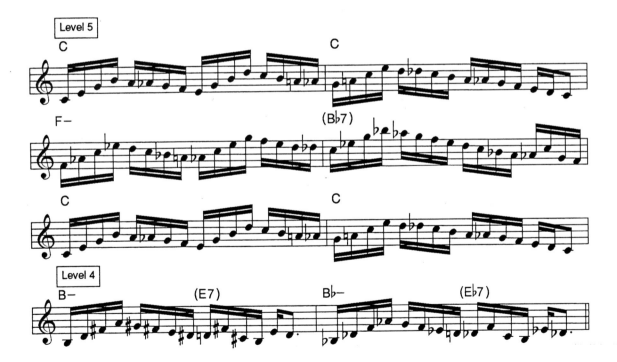

The following example shows how the player might combine these exercises for practice purposes.

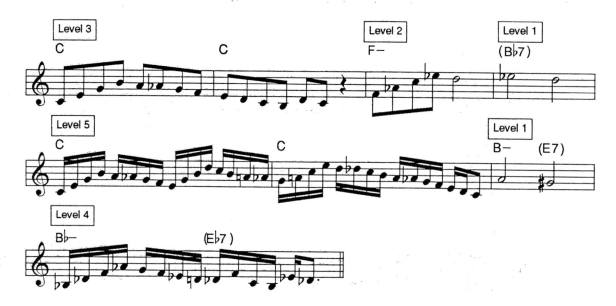

CHAPTER VII

Practicing Changes on "Three Levels"

In this approach the player is encouraged to think on one of three different overlapping levels in creating an improvisation.

Level One. This level uses the major scale to realize all of the chords in a tune. This allows only the smallest amount of information about the changes, as in the following example:

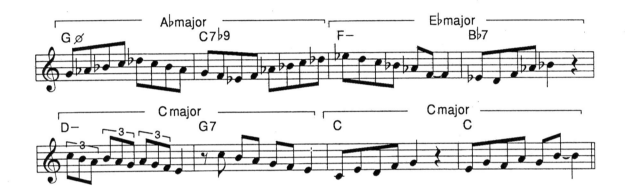

Level Two. On this level only the II V7 are affected: Both the II and V are treated as a II V progression, as in the following example:

| | D- | | D- | | = | | D- | | G7 | |
| G7 | | G7 | | = | | D- | | G7 | |

Treat the V7 as a II chord, as in the following example:

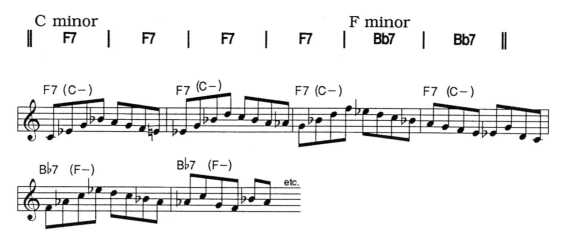

Level Three. This is the V chord level and is the level of highest specificity. It is applicable only in the II V7 situation, as in the following example:

| D- | G7 | = | G7 | G7 |

Maximum possibilities exist at this level, as illustrated by the following examples:

G7 = mixolydian, bebop dominant

G7(#11) = lydian dominant

G7(#5) = whole tone

G7(b9) = diminished

G7(#9#5) = diminished whole tone

Also, various other appropriate scales including pentatonics can be used.

Practicing the Levels

Level One. Practice Level One on virtually any II-V-I situation (almost any pop, standard or bebop tune).

Level Two. Practice Level Two on a plain old blues ("Now's the Time" and others)

Level Three. Practice Level Three on modal tunes ("So What," "Maiden Voyage"), bebop tunes ("Confirmation," "Groovin' High"), or with the minor tracks on the Major/Minor play-a-long (Jamey Aebersold, vol. 24). Practice imposing the various genre scales on the minor chords.

Few experienced players play exclusively on one level, with the possible exception of Level Three. I encourage you to practice playing on any one of the three levels on command. Practice this approach on a wide variety of tunes using the play-a-long records. If you have trouble, start with the simpler modal tunes.

CHAPTER VIII

Practicing Changes: The "Twice-As-Long" Song

For this exercise pick a tune that moves in two or four measure groups of changes. Many bebop and standard tunes would be appropriate choices, such as "Half Nelson," "Take the 'A' Train," "Groovin' High," "Getting Sentimental Over You," "Woody'n You," "Hot House," and others. "Half Nelson" is the tune that will be used to exemplify this approach.

Here are the changes to the first eight measures of "Half Nelson."

‖C |C |F– |Bb7 |C |C |B– E7 |Bb– Eb7 ‖

Now make each two measure group of changes last twice as long.

‖C |C |C |C |F– |Bb7 | F– | Bb7 | etc.

Using the first two measures, sing a phrase which lasts the length of the chord change; sing it exactly as you would like it to sound (time feel, articulation, etc.). Then repeat the chord in those two measures and play the same phrase, repeating it as often as necessary until it sounds exactly like you sang it.

34

Strive to play what you would sing, not sing what you would play. Don't sing your patterns, clichés, etc.; sing what you hear, not what your fingers know!

If you don't have access to a live rhythm section for the purpose of practicing this exercise, I strongly suggest that you go to the piano or some other chordal instrument and make yourself a play-a-long.

For variety, practice this exercise with another player. Practice it as a game; play "Horse" or "Rat" as in basketball. Try to stump each other. Use double-time, push the range, vary the articulation, throw rhythmic curves, add substitutions and turnarounds, use different scales, etc.

Your goal is to hear everything before you play it. Start with simple ideas. Don't be afraid to fail. Persevere.

CHAPTER IX

Tune Learning Strategies

One way to invigorate the practice of tune learning is to focus on a single category of tunes on a given day during a given practice period. Some possible tune categories are as follows:

1. Standards

2. Bebop tunes

3. Contemporary tunes

4. Blues

5. "I Got Rhythm" tunes

6. Tunes that use the same basic formula

7. Tunes of a single composer (Monk, Ellington, Jerome Kern, Cole Porter, Tadd Dameron, et al)

8. Tunes originally in the same key ("Body and Soul," "Stardust," and "Zing Went the Strings of My Heart" are all in Db.)

9. Tunes from the same show

   Oklahoma
   •"O What a Beautiful Morning"
   •"Surrey with the Fringe on Top"
   •"I'm Just a Girl Who Can't Say No"
   •etc.

   Porgy and Bess
   •"Summertime"
   •"I Loves You Porgy"
   •"It Ain't Necessarily So"
   •etc.

10. Tunes associated with the same performing artist (Miles Davis, Ahmad Jamal, Cannonball Adderley, Charlie Parker, etc.)

11. Tunes associated by title

    Spring
    •"Spring Is Here"
    •"It Might As Well Be Spring"
    •"Spring Can Really Hang You Up the Most"
    •"Spring Will Be a Little Late This Year"

<u>Love</u>
- "Love Is Just Around the Corner"
- "Love"
- "I Love You"
- "Let's Fall in Love"
- "If I Loved You"

<u>April</u>
- "April in Paris"
- "I'll Remember April"
- "April Love"
- "Lost April"
- etc.

12. All the contrafacts on a given tune (see chapter 1 in <u>How To Play</u> <u>Bebop, vol. 3</u> by David Baker)

    <u>"What Is This Thing Called Love"</u>
    - "Barry's Bop"
    - "Hot House"
    - "100 Proof"
    - "Flat Black"
    - "Subconscious-lee"
    - "No Figs"
    - etc.

13. Tunes linked by meters other than 4/4

14. The tune you didn't know last night

Another way to invigorate the practice of tune learning is to explore an individual tune in the following ways:

1. Play a single two or four measure phrase through all keys.

2. Play complete sections (eight or 16 bars) through all keys.

3. Play the entire tune through all keys.

4. For recall purposes and complete comfort with the compositions:

    a Start the tune from various places in the form, e.g., the fourth measure, the fifth measure, the seventh measure, etc.

    b. Play the bridge through all the keys.

    c. On a given day start each tune on the same starting note, irrespective of key. For example, using the starting note C, "Misty" would be in the key of F, "Gettin' Sentimental Over You" would be in the key of Db, "Somewhere Over the Rainbow" would be in the key of C, etc.

d. Start each new tune on the last note of the previous tune.

e. Take each successive phrase up by half-steps, whole steps, minor thirds, major thirds, fourths, etc.

f. Take any two, four, six, or eight measure set of changes and try to recall/sing/play as many tune fragments as you can conjure up that fit that progression. Interchange these melodies in various situations. Transpose them to fit the situation, as in the following example:

Bridge of "Joy Spring"

‖ C | C- F7 | Bb | Bb- Eb7 | Ab ‖

A section of "Afternoon in Paris"

‖ C | C- F7 | Bb | Bb- Eb7 | Ab ‖

A section of "The End of a Love Affair"

‖ C- F7 | Bb | Bb- Eb7 | Ab ‖

CHAPTER X

A Practice Technique for Using Bebop Tunes as a Tool for Learning and Internalizing the Bebop Language

In Appendix A (page 59) you will find a list of 55 bebop tunes. These particular tunes were chosen because each contains several melodic/harmonic patterns which have endured over the years and still enjoy high currency among today's jazz musicians. The patterns in these tunes comprise a substantial portion of the language of every important jazz player since the ascendancy of Dizzy Gillespie and Charlie Parker.

As you practice your way through these 55 bebop tunes, you will find yourself growing at an unprecedented rate of speed, particularly if over the next few months or the next year you internalize the tunes in the manner described in this chapter. Your ultimate goal should be the memorization and internalization of as many bebop tunes as possible. It is essential that you practice these exercises with play-a-long recordings; commercial recordings; a rhythm section; and, especially, solo.

The first step in this process is learning the melody of the tune in question and being able to reproduce it accurately. For illustrative purposes the tune we will use is "Half Nelson" by Miles Davis.

Next, take each phrase and apply it to the entire tune as in examples A, B, and C. In example A the melody to "Half Nelson" is used in measures 1 and 2. The pattern uses the notes of a major scale and starts on the fifth of the home key. (Be sure to figure the home key of the II V7 measures, e.g., F- Bb7 = Eb major.)

Example B uses measures 3 and 4 of "Half Nelson." The pattern uses the notes of the major scale and starts on the fifth of the home key.

Example C uses measures 9 and 10 of "Half Nelson." The pattern uses the notes of the major scale and starts on the seventh of the home key.

Next transpose each phrase of "Half Nelson" to the key of C
(examples D through I).

Measures 7 and 8 are special in that the II V7 progression is
approached from a half-step above, as in the following example:

| B– E7 | Bb – Eb7 |

substitutes for

| Bb– | Eb7 |

Example J transposes this substitution to a II V in the key of C.

Measures 15 and 16 (example K) are also special in that this progression occurs only as a turnback. (see chapter 6: "The Use of the Turnback in Bebop" in <u>How to Play Bebop, vol. 2</u> by David Baker)

Now take each phrase through all keys. Finally, play the entire tune in all 12 keys. Once you're comfortable with this approach, proceed to the other 54 tunes on the bebop **must** list (Appendix A, page 59).

With each new tune bring all of the melodic material from the previous tunes, as in examples L, M, and N.

Example L uses the changes to "Groovin' High" in combination with material from "Half Nelson."

Example M uses a mixture of melodic material from both "Half Nelson" and "Groovin' High."

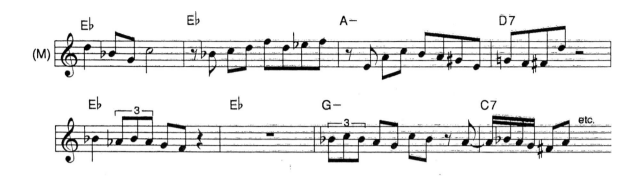

Example N uses the changes to "Half Nelson" in combination with melodic material from "Half Nelson," "Groovin' High," and "Hot House."

CHAPTER XI

Transcribing as a Practice/Study Technique

In the years before jazz instruction was formalized, jazz players learned to play in a variety of ways. The transcription of solos was one of the most efficient and practiced ways of learning the jazz language. More often than not the aspiring improviser eschewed the practice of writing these solos down, opting for memorizing the specific solo or portion thereof. Eliminating this intermediate step forced the player to come to grips with the material first hand.

In the halcyon days of bebop (pre-LPs and CDs) I wore out many a 78 recording learning the latest J.J. Johnson solos. The modus operandi was to play the recording until I could sing the solo one phrase at a time, chorus after chorus until I could finally sing the entire solo. At this point I would begin the arduous but exciting and ultimately rewarding task of committing the solo to the horn. After years of learning the solos of my hero and favorite trombonist I realized that I began to be able to anticipate to some degree what his musical choices might be in a given situation: the tempo, the key, the changes, the mood of the piece, the musical environment (rhythm section, other participants, time limitations). I would later realize that the learning process that I was employing was being replicated by players everywhere.

As a teacher I have tried to have my students replicate this procedure with specific guidelines to expedite and enhance the learning process. The student and I choose a soloist on the student's instrument and together we determine how long the period of study with the chosen giant will be (usually 4-6 weeks). Our goal is to allow the student the opportunity to "study" with the recordings of a player of his/her own choosing.

Learning the Solo

1. Play the head and solo. Match tone quality, articulation, and every other aspect of the player's performance.

2. At first don't be too concerned with being analytical; just match everything including blemishes, intonation peculiarities, and phrasing.

3. Repetition is the mother of memory! Play phrases over and over until it is impossible to distinguish your sound from the recording. If necessary, work the solos at half speed until all of your mentor's nuances and mannerisms are perfected.

Analyzing the Solo

1. When listening to the solo, try to determine the following:

    •Which II V7 patterns, cycles, turnbacks, quotes, or scale choices recur?
    •In what sequence?
    •Which ones occur only in certain keys or on certain changes?
    •Which ones occur at certain tempos?
    •Does the player use double-time, etc.?
    •What are the preferred substitution choices?

2. To ascertain how the player uses certain scales and patterns try to find tunes on which he is likely to use:

    a   a certain scale, as in the following examples:
    •D7+5 (whole tone scale, third bar of "Take the 'A' Train")
    •Bb-Δ (Bb ascending melodic minor scale, first measure of "Nica's Dream")
    •C7b9 (diminished scale, first 12 measures of "Caravan")

    b.   a certain pattern, as in the following examples:
    •"Jordu" (the entire tune is a cycle)
    •"Half Nelson" (turnbacks)

    You can, of course, figure out the changes that are being used on the tunes you are transcribing and elicit the same information.

3. Begin to look for tendencies, such as the following:

    a   Does the player tend to start phrases on an upbeat?

    b.   Does he/she end a solo in a neat and orderly fashion on the downbeat of the next chorus or the downbeat of the tonic chord?

    c.   Does the soloist begin his/her solos with a pre-set idea such as a quote or a favorite lick or pattern?

    d.   Does the soloist tend to develop the last idea or an earlier idea of the previous soloist?

    e.   Does the soloist tend to start a solo at the tension level of the previous soloist or back off in order to build from scratch?

    f.   Does the soloist use dynamics? If so, how? Sudden changes? Gradual changes?

    g.   Study sound, attack, and articulation.

h.   Study mannerisms. For example, on saxophone study vent fingering, airy sound, and slurs; and on trumpet half valves and unusual tonguing

i.   Observe favorite tessitura and range.

j.   Study time feel, including what kind of eighth notes: even, slurred, uneven, swing, cute, on top, laid-back, lots of space.

k.   Observe tune preferences, tempo preferences, key, etc.

l.   Observe the degree of specificity with regard to the realization of the changes.

m.   Study formulae such as turnbacks, cycles, midrange patterns, and short patterns.

4.   Examine the broader considerations:

a   broad gestures versus detail and minutiae

b.   thematic playing (Thelonious Monk, J.J. Johnson, Sonny Rollins, John Lewis) versus change running (Sonny Stitt, John Coltrane)

c.   use of quotation, repetition, scale exhaustion

5.   Next try to find a recording of a tune that you have not transcribed or heard by the soloist. Tape yourself playing on those changes and at that tempo and compare it with the actual solo by your subject. Repeat the learning stages until your solos are virtually indistinguishable from your adopted "mentor."

6.   Now go on to another soloist but choose one a distance away in style from the first. For example, if the first soloist was Sonny Rollins, try John Coltrane, Dexter Gordon, or Stan Getz as your next project.

The objective in the preceding routine is to provide the aspiring player the opportunity to study with as many of the giants of his/her instrument as time, energy, and ingenuity permit.

Once the player is comfortable with these techniques, he/she might profitably pick players who play a different instrument. This will, of course, mean replication at a lower level of specificity with regard to matching the idiosyncrasies of other instruments.

Refer to the Giants of Jazz series by David Baker for a modus operandi. The volumes in this series include:

•Cannonball Adderley   •Miles Davis
•Clifford Brown   •Fats Navarro
•John Coltrane   •Sonny Rollins

46

CHAPTER XII

Practicing with Play-A-Longs

Play-a-long recordings, particularly those in the Jamey Aebersold Series, fall into one of several, often overlapping categories:

1. those that feature the compositions of a single pop or jazz composer (e.g., Jerome Kern, Thelonious Monk, Charlie Parker, Miles Davis, Duke Ellington and John Coltrane)

2. those that feature the compositions of several composers (e.g., 13 Favorite Standards, One Dozen Standards, All Time Standards, etc.)

3. those that feature the much used forms of blues (e.g., Nothin' but Blues and Minor Blues in All Keys) and rhythm   (I Got Rhythm)

4. those designed to foster the development of jazz language skills (e.g. Jazz: How to Play and Improvise, The II/V7/I Progression, Turnarounds, Cycles and II/V7's, Major and Minor, etc.)

For practice purposes the compositions on play-a-long recordings in the first and second categories are most effectively approached in the following manner:

1. Memorize melody and changes

2. Develop some standardized routine for maximizing the effectiveness of your practice.

    a   Play the melody.

    b.   Play through the changes using roots only.

    c.   Play resolving tones through the changes.

    d.   Play generic patterns. (see chapter VI, page 27)

    e.   Play double time generic patterns. (see chapter VI, page 27)

    f.   Play your pattern or patterns of the day or week.

    g.   Use the melodic and rhythmic materials indigenous to the tune itself.

    h.   Isolate and use different genre scales, either exclusively or in combination. (see chapter II, page 4 and chapter VII, page 31)

i. When applicable, practice the melodies to appropriate contrafacts.

j. Write, memorize, and improvise new melodies on the changes.

k. Play the various etudes written to be played with specific play-a-longs. (see Aebersold _Jazz Aids_ catalogue)

l. Play transcribed solos (your own or published ones) with the appropriate play-a-longs.

m. Play the changes using the melody exclusively as the guide and point of departure.

n. Sing solos!

o. Sing solos, tape them and then transcribe what you sing.

This approach excludes modal tunes, blues and rhythm changes.

For practicing with the blues and rhythm play-a-longs I strongly suggest the approach outlined in chapter 7: "Another Approach to Learning to Improvise on the Blues" and chapter 8: "An Approach to Improvising on Rhythm Tunes" in _How to Play Bebop, vol. 3_ by David Baker.

Use the major tracks from Volume 24 (_Major and Minor_) of the Aebersold Play-A-Longs to practice bebop major scales, Lydian scale melodies, and quotes based on major melodies. Practice with the various tracks concentrating on:

•swing, latin, or rock feel, whatever is appropriate
•intonation
•technique
•articulation
•accuracy
•anything else that would require scale practice

Use the minor tracks on Volume 24 to practice various scales which can be used to color the G minor seventh chord, such as G dorian, G blues, G and other pentatonics, G ascending melodic minor, C bebop, C whole tone, C diminished, C diminished whole tone, F major, or Bb lydian augmented.

Keep in mind that many of the scale choices listed above will sound very foreign to the ear at first, but they are legitimate and often used alternatives.

Use Volume 3, Volume 16, and virtually any of the song-oriented play-a-longs to practice the following:

•II V7 I	•the most commonly used formulae
•cycles	•generic patterns
•turnbacks	•other public domain patterns

CHAPTER XIII

How to Practice with Actual Recordings

In the not so distant past, before the advent of Music Minus One and Play-A-Longs, aspiring players used their jazz records not only for the purpose of playing along with the solos of their player of choice, but also for the opportunity to be accompanied by the rhythm section on the record in question. In this instance the player would play a solo of his/her own as a parallel solo to the one on the record, playing a kind of counterpoint or interaction with the soloist and/or the rhythm section and often playing parts of the solo in question when desired. What a thrill playing with a rhythm section of Bud Powell, Ray Brown and Max Roach, or John Lewis, Tommy Potter and Kenny Clarke, et al!

Today's players can choose from a wealth of available records, tapes and CDs. I suggest that whatever your instrument (particularly melody instruments) you develop the habit of learning and memorizing harmony parts directly from the record. For example, learn the melody line and the second part on Horace Silver's "Nica's Dream," or all the horn parts on the Blakey quintets/sextets, or all the horn parts on a Tristano septet recording. (Learning the inner parts becomes impractical if there are more than three or four horns.) Don't write the parts down; memorize them directly from recordings. The benefits should be obvious. In the real world you will often have to learn a lot of music in a short period of time when, for instance, you replace one of the horn players in a working group, usually without the benefit of extensive rehearsal time.

The following is a list of some groups with suitable tunes for practicing learning inner voices:

•Miles Davis Sextet (Vol. I, Blue Note 1501)
•Miles Davis Sextet with Coltrane and Cannonball
•Miles Davis quintets with Coltrane
•Max Roach/Clifford Brown quintets
•Clifford Brown sextet with J.J. Johnson and Jimmy Heath
•The Horace Silver quintets and sextet
•Any Jazz Messenger recording
•Any recording of The Jazztet
•Quintet and sextet recordings by any of the jazz giants

CHAPTER XIV

"The Game"
A Practice Strategy

Rationale for "The Game"

Practice the game to:

- learn a large number of disparate melodies
- develop instant recall
- train ear-to-hand skills that allow you to instantly play what you hear
- foster rapid and accurate identification of intervallic sequences
- foster the ability to instantly transpose entire melodies or portions thereof to different keys dictated by the changes
- train the ear to hear and the mind to think in this relatively unorthodox manner
- develop the ability to change the musical environment and matrix

Rules of "The Game"

1. Two or more players can participate.

2. The first player plays four or eight measures of a tune (jazz, pop, standard, folk, non-jazz, etc.).

3. The next player has a time limit (15 or 30 seconds) to respond by taking the last two different pitches of the first player's tune and using those two pitches to start another tune. He plays four or eight measures and the next player responds as the second player did.

4. The player must start with the identical pitches from the end of the preceding player's phrase; this helps to develop his sense of relative pitch.

An example of how to play the game with four players follows on the next page.

The players should prepare for the game by learning the opening interval of as many tunes (in all idioms) as possible. The following tunes, for example, all begin with an ascending half-step:

1. "What's New"
2. "Getting Sentimental Over You"
3. "Serenade in Blue"
4. "Early Autumn"
5. "I Remember You"
6. "Fascination"
7. "You and the Night and the Music"

For maximum benefit the players should make an effort to learn as many tunes in their entirety as possible. Ideally, to function properly in this game, players need to be able to play the melodies in all keys. The players must work diligently to break free of tonal restrictions that might prevent them from hearing intervals in an unrestricted way. For example, in the musical example given on how to play the game, the first player played "Twinkle, Twinkle Little Star." The last interval of that line is 2 to 1 in the key of C, but the second player's line ("Three Blind Mice") begins 3 to 2 in the key of Bb. The pitches in both examples are the same (D followed by C) and if the ear persists in hearing the first key area, it will prevent the mind from functioning unimpaired in hearing 3 to 2 in the new key and will insist on trying to find a phrase that moves 2 to 1 as in "Twinkle, Twinkle Little Star."

51

The player may choose to organize the newly learned tunes in various ways such as by genre, style, tempo, title, composer, etc. The following examples are organized by genre:

Bebop Tunes Beginning with an Ascending Perfect Fourth

1. "Anthropology"
2. "Dexterity"
3. "Good Bait"
4. "Little Willie Leaps"
5. "Joy Spring"
   etc.

Standards Beginning with an Ascending Perfect Fourth

1. "The Nearness of You"
2. "How High the Moon"
3. "The Shadow of Your Smile"
4. "Again"
5. "All God's Children Got Rhythm"
6. "The Breeze and I"
   etc.

Blues Beginning with an Ascending Perfect Fourth

1. "Straight No Chaser"
2. "Now the Time"
   etc.

Expanding "The Game"

If you want to make the game more interesting and difficult, try the following:

1. Specify a shorter length of time in which to respond.
2. Limit the new tune by source, as in the following categories:

   a. tunes from musicals (Broadway)
   b. tunes from movies
   c. tunes from operas, symphonies, concertos, cantatas, etc.
   d. tunes by a specific composer - e.g., Ellington, Monk, Parker, Dizzy, Dameron, Miles, Bach, Beethoven, Brahms, Debussy, Dvorak, etc.

3.   Instead of using the last two pitches of the previous player's tune, use the last three pitches. Using three or four notes becomes decidedly more difficult because opening phrases are very different from melodic cadential formulae. The following example uses the end of the first phrase of "Over the Rainbow."

"Over The Rainbow"

Here are some examples of tunes that could be used by the next player:

"Dear Old Stockholm"

"Unfinished Symphony"

"Autumn Leaves"

"Limehouse Blues"

CHAPTER XV

Practicing Performing

Each day at some point <u>practice performing</u>! Here are some ways to incorporate this into your routine.

1. Simulate performance conditions - for example, play without stopping to make corrections.

2. Play an entire composition:
   head - solo - backgrounds - head - ending

3. Once in a long while force yourself to play with very little or no warm-up. Occasions will arise when conditions will not be optimum and you will have to perform without sufficient preparation time. Plan for the unplanned!

4. Play alone, with others, with a play-a-long, or with actual recordings.

5. Pick a program (long or short) and perform for an imaginary audience.

The Performance: Some Suggestions

1. Communicate; that's the objective.

2. Play at performance level volume.

3. In your mind, create ways to interact with your imaginary accompanying group. (This is, of course, a lot easier when playing with an actual group or a recording.)

4. Play with confidence, flair, style and imagination.

5. Think time! Play in the correct style - swing, Latin, rock, free, etc.

6. If you choose to play in a bebop or post bebop tradition or other circumstance when a faithful rendition of the changes is the objective, then the listener, at least at the outset, should be able to recognize the changes from the solo's content with or without a rhythm section or the accompanying melody. The use of leading tones, proper chord alterations, and nods or allusions to the underlying form all will contribute to your success in achieving the desired results. Your goal is being faithful to the changes while avoiding being predictable and obvious.

7. You might find it helpful to imagine your ideas as characters in a drama. Using all of your expressive resources, subject the characters to different treatment via contrasting various elements such as vibrato, registration, volume, articulation, speed and other musical gestures.

8.   Always strive to bring a clear and well-articulated but fresh and individual viewpoint to the solo specifically and to the performance in general. This objective might be achieved by manipulating various components, among them the following:

   a.   The changes. Use substitutions, chord alterations, vamps, pedalpoints, etc.

   b.   The time. Use half-time, double-time, metric modulation, playing freely over the underlying beat, etc.

   c.   The original theme itself or an original melody of your own invention. Use inversion, diminution, truncation, elongation, fragmentation, or some less formal technique(s).

   d.   The mood. Vary the mood of the improvisation - e.g., bright, playful, brooding, etc. (whatever these and other descriptive terms convey to you).

9.   The more conventional, ordinary and predictable the situation is with regard to changes, form, tempo, etc., the greater the necessity for avoiding the obvious and vice versa.

Recommended Reading

Baker, David. Chapter XIX: "A Psychological Approach to Communication Through an Improvised Solo," pp. 113-115 in Jazz Improvisation: A Comprehensive Method of Study for All Players. Revised edition. Bloomington, IN: Frangipani Press, 1983. Currently published by Alfred Publishing Company (Van Nuys, CA).

Meyer, Leonard B. Chapter 2: "Some Remarks on Value and Greatness in Music," pp. 22-41 in Music, The Arts and Ideas: Patterns and Predictions in Twentieth-Century Culture. Chicago: University of Chicago Press: 1967.

CHAPTER XVI

Practicing Reading Skills Using Transcribed Solos

The following is an exercise designed to improve your reading skills through the use of transcribed solos.

For this exercise you will need:

> •written transcriptions (either your own or those which are commercially available, such as those in The Charlie Parker Omnibook or various volumes of David Baker's Giants of Jazz series)

> •a tape machine with a 1/2 speed capability

How to proceed:

1. Choose written transcriptions for which you have recordings (tapes).

2. At 1/2 speed memorize the recorded solo (or a portion thereof) by ear, without consulting the music.

3. Play the memorized solo (or portion of the solo) along with the recording while looking at the written notes. Observe dynamics, phrasing, and articulation.

4. As you become more comfortable, "read" the solo without the recording, gradually speeding it up. Use a metronome to chart your progress.

5. Practice "reading" the solo with the tune at actual speed.

6. Practice this exercise using a wide variety of transcribed solos encompassing different styles, eras, and instrumentalists.

This exercise is not intended to supplant your regular sight-reading exercises but to serve as a practical supplement to them.

CHAPTER XVII

Improving Your Reading Using Fakebooks

For these exercises you will need:

- •a supply of fakebooks with the melodies written out. The Jamey Aebersold Play-A-Long books are excellent for these exercises.

- •a metronome

Exercise #1

    a   Choose tunes to which you know the melody reasonably well.

    b.   Play them slowly with the metronome. Read <u>exactly</u> what is written, <u>especially</u> if it is different from what you are used to hearing rhythmically and melodically.

    c.   Try to read at least ten such tunes a day, gradually moving toward a correct tempo.

Exercise #2

    a   Choose tunes that you know vaguely or simply have heard and "kind of" recognize.

    b.   As before, play the tunes slowly and with absolute accuracy according to the printed page. Gradually work toward doing this at the suggested tempo.

    c.   Play ten or more tunes daily.

Exercise #3

    Choose unfamiliar tunes and follow the same regimen.

    Gradually you will be able to read and play tunes accurately and at tempo the first time. Try reading the melodies with the accompanying Play-A-Longs.

CHAPTER XVIII

Evaluating Your Playing

1. Whenever possible tape your practices or performances for periodic post-practice and post-performance evaluation. A very revealing exercise is to tape yourself playing on a particular set of changes with a rhythm section, play-a-long or solo. A week, month, or a year later play along with your recorded solo and notice how frequently you end up playing the same ideas in the same sequence as before!

2. Try to determine what was or wasn't working and why.

   a. Are there too many scale passages? If so, practice breaking the scales up in unpredictable ways. (see chapter II: "Imaginative Scale Practicing," page 4)

   b. Do you overuse a scale of a particular genre? Do you use certain scales in a predictable sequence? Forewarned is forearmed.

   c. When you play certain ideas do they always evoke the same consequence?

   d. Are there too many public domain ideas? Too few public domain ideas? Strive for some kind of balance.

3. Strive for a beautiful, controlled tone. Remember, this is the first thing a listener hears when you play. Strive constantly and diligently to reach a point where you can fit your sound to the content.

4. Do you use too many or too few ideas per chorus? Are the ideas followed through to completion?

5. Is your time good? If not, try to determine if it is a metronomic problem or a problem with the placement of melody notes. If you use the bebop scale and the chord tones do not fall on down beats, the illusion is that the metronomic time is bad. (see How To Play Bebop, vol. 1 by David Baker)

6. To put it bluntly, do you know when to end a solo? Always stop while you still have more to say.

7. Don't underestimate the value and power of silence.

8. Finally, if you are to successfully communicate your ideas to others they must first be clear in your own mind.

APPENDIX A

A LIST OF ESSENTIAL BEBOP TUNES FOR MEMORIZATION

1. Afternoon in Paris...John Lewis
2. Anthropology ....Dizzy Gillespie
3. Back Home Blues ....Charlie Parker
4. Barbados ....Charlie Parker
5. Bebop..Dizzy Gillespie
6. Bebop Revisited...David Baker
7. Billie's Bounce...Charlie Parker
8. Birdlike ....Freddie Hubbard
9. Bloomdido ....Charlie Parker
10. Bouncin' with Bud ....Bud Powell
11. Brownie Speaks..Clifford Brown
12. Calcutta Cutie ....Horace Silver
13. Cheryl...Charlie Parker
14. Chi-Chi ....Charlie Parker
15. Confirmation...Charlie Parker
16. Cookin' at the Continental ....Horace Silver
17. Dance of the Infidels..Bud Powell
18. Dewey Square...Charlie Parker
19. Dexterity ....Charlie Parker
20. Donna ....Jackie McLean
21. Donna Lee ....Charlie Parker
22. Don't Argue ....Kai Winding
23. Eternal Triangle..Sonny Stitt

24. Four Brothers ....Jimmy Giuffre

25. Good Bait ....Tadd Dameron

26. Groovin' High ....Dizzy Gillespie

27. Half Nelson ....Miles Davis

28. Hot House ....Tadd Dameron

29. Jordu ....Duke Jordan

30. Joy Spring ....Clifford Brown

31. Little Willie Leaps ....Charlie Parker

32. Mayreh ....Horace Silver

33. Milestones (old) ....Miles Davis

34. Mohawk ....Charlie Parker

35. Moose the Mooche ....Charlie Parker

36. A Night in Tunisia ....Dizzy Gillespie

37. Opus V ....J.J. Johnson

38. Ornithology ....Benny Harris

39. Passport ....Charlie Parker

40. Relaxin' at Camarillo ....Charlie Parker

41. Quicksilver ....Horace Silver

42. Room 608 ....Horace Silver

43. Salt Peanuts (entire tune) ....Dizzy Gillespie

44. Scrapple from the Apple ....Charlie Parker

45. The Serpent's Tooth ....Miles Davis

46. Shaw Nuff...Dizzy Gillespie
                                                                                                                    Charlie Parker

47. Sippin' at Bells ....Miles Davis

48. Split Kick ....Horace Silver

49. Steeplechase ....Charlie Parker

50. That's Earl, Brother...Gil Fuller

51. Things to Come ....Dizzy Gillespie

52. Wail..Bud Powell

53. Where You At?..Horace Silver

54. Woody 'N' You ....Dizzy Gillespie

55. Yardbird Suite ....Charlie Parker

APPENDIX B

BIBLIOGRAPHY

I. References Cited in the Text

Baker, David. How To Play Bebop, vol. 1. The Bebop Scale and Other Scales in Common Use. Bloomington, IN: Frangipani Press, 1985. Currently published by Alfred Publishing Company (Van Nuys, CA).

_____. How To Play Bebop, vol. 2. Learning the Bebop Language: Patterns, Formulae and Other Linking Materials. Bloomington, IN: Frangipani Press, 1985. Currently published by Alfred Publishing Company (Van Nuys, CA).

_____. How To Play Bebop, vol. 3. Techniques for Learning and Utilizing Bebop Tunes. Bloomington, IN: Frangipani Press, 1985. Currently published by Alfred Publishing Company (Van Nuys, CA).

_____. Jazz Improvisation: A Comprehensive Method of Study for All Players. Revised edition. Bloomington, IN: Frangipani Press, 1983. Currently published by Alfred Publishing Company (Van Nuys, CA).

_____. Giants of Jazz series. Six volumes, as follows:

The Jazz Style of Clifford Brown: A Musical and Historical Perspective. Lebanon, IN: Studio PR, 1982. Currently published by Columbia Pictures Publications/Belwin Mills (Miami, FL).

The Jazz Style of Fats Navarro: A Musical and Historical Perspective. Lebanon, IN: Studio PR, 1982. Currently published by Columbia Pictures Publications/Belwin Mills (Miami, FL).

The Jazz Style of John Coltrane: A Musical and Historical Perspective. Lebanon, IN: Studio PR, 1980. Currently published by Columbia Pictures Publications/Belwin Mills (Miami, FL).

The Jazz Style of Julian "Cannonball" Adderley: A Musical and Historical Perspective. Lebanon, IN: Studio PR, 1980. Currently published by Columbia Pictures Publications/Belwin Mills (Miami, FL).

The Jazz Style of Miles Davis: A Musical and Historical Perspective. Lebanon, IN: Studio PR, 1980. Currently published by Columbia Pictures Publications/Belwin Mills (Miami, FL).

The Jazz Style of Sonny Rollins: A Musical and Historical Perspective. Lebanon, IN: Studio PR, 1980. Currently published by Columbia Pictures Publications/Belwin Mills (Miami, FL).

Meyer, Leonard. <u>Music, the Arts and Ideas: Patterns and Predictions in Twentieth-Century Culture</u>. Chicago: University of·Chicago Press, 1967.

Slone, Ken. <u>The Charlie Parker Omnibook</u>. Atlantic Music Corp., 1978.

II. Recommended Reading

Allen, Margaret. <u>Guides to Creative Motion Musicianship</u>. Ardmore, PA: Dorrance & Company, 1970.

Covey, Stephen R. <u>The 7 Habits of Highly Effective People</u>. New York: Simon & Schuster, 1989.

Gardner, Howard. <u>Creating Minds: An Anatomy of Creativity Seen Through the Lives of Freud, Einstein, Picasso, Stravinsky, Eliot, Graham, and Gandhi</u>. New York: BasicBooks, HarperCollins, 1993.

_____. <u>Frames of Mind: The Theory of Multiple Intelligences</u>. New York: Basic Books, 1983.

Hindemith, Paul. <u>Elementary Training for Musicians</u>. 2nd ed. New York: Schott Music Corp., 1949.

Johnson, Spencer. <u>One Minute for Myself</u>. New York: Avon Books, 1985.

Klatzky, Roberta L. <u>Human Memory: Structures and Processes</u>. San Francisco: W.H. Freeman and Company, 1975.

Koestler, Arthur. <u>The Act of Creation</u>. New York: The Macmillan Company, 1964.

Lieberman, Julie Lyonn. <u>You Are Your Instrument: The Definitive Musician's Guide to Practice and Performance</u>. New York: Huiksi Music, 1991.

Minninger, Joan. <u>Total Recall: How to Boost Your Memory Power</u>. Emmaus, PA: Rodale Press, 1984.

Nachmanovitch, Stephen. <u>Free Play: The Power of Improvisation in Life and Art</u>. Los Angeles: Jeremy P. Tarcher, Inc., 1990.

Perkins, D.N. <u>The Mind's Best Work</u>. Cambridge, MA: Harvard University Press, 1981.

Risenhoover, Morris and Blackburn, Robert T. <u>Artists As Professors: Conversations with Musicians, Painters, Sculptors</u>. Urbana,: University of Illinois Press, 1976.

III. Other Books by David Baker

Advanced Ear Training for the Jazz Musician. Lebanon, IN: Studio PR, 1977. Currently published by Columbia Pictures Publications/Belwin Mills (Miami, FL)

Advanced Improvisation. Chicago: Maher Publications, 1974. Currently published in 2 volumes by Alfred Publishing Company (Van Nuys, CA). 1. Improvisational Concepts; 2. Rhythmic and Melodic Concepts.

Arranging and Composing for the Small Ensemble: Jazz/R&B/Jazz-Rock. Revised edition. Bloomington, IN: Frangipani Press, 1985. Currently published by Alfred Publishing Company (Van Nuys, CA)

Bebop Jazz Solos: Correlated with Volumes 10 and 13 of Jamey Aebersold's Play-A-Long Book and Record Series. Treble clef, bass clef, Bb, and Eb editions. New Albany, IN: Jamey Aebersold, 1981.

Contemporary Patterns. Treble clef and bass clef editions. New York: Charles Colin, 1979.

Contemporary Techniques for the Trombone. 2 volumes. New York: Charles Colin, 1974.

David Baker's Jazz Monograph Series. Charlie Parker: Alto Saxophone. New York: Shattinger International Music Corp., 1978.

David Bakers's Jazz Monograph Series. J.J. Johnson: Trombone. New York: Shattinger International Music Corp., 1978.

Ear Training for Jazz Musicians. 5 volumes. 1. Intervals; 2. Triads/Three Note Sets/Four and Five Note Sets; 3. Seventh Chords/Scales; 4. Major Melodies/Turnarounds/I VI7 Formulae;
5. II V7 Patterns. Lebanon, IN: Studio PR, 1981. Currently published by Columbia Pictures Publications/Belwin Mills (Miami, FL).

Improvisational Patterns: The Bebop Era. 3 volumes. Treble clef and bass clef editions. New York: Charles Colin, 1979.

Improvisational Patterns: The Blues. Treble clef and bass clef editions. New York: Charles Colin, 1980.

Jazz Etudes: Correlated with Volumes 5 & 6 of Jamey Aebersold's Play-A-Long Book and Record Series. Treble clef, bass clef, Bb, and Eb editions. New Albany, IN: Jamey Aebersold, 1979.

Jazz Improvisation: A Comprehensive Method of Study for All Players. Revised edition. Bloomington, IN: Frangipani Press, 1983. Currently published by Alfred Publishing Company (Van Nuys, CA).

Jazz Improvisation: Eine umfassende Methode fur alle Instrumente. Rottenburg, West Germany: Advance Music.

A Jazz Improvisation Method for Stringed Instruments. 2 volumes. 1. Violin and Viola; 2. Cello and Bass Viol. Chicago: Maher Publications, 1976. Currently published by Alfred Publishing Company (Van Nuys, CA).

Jazz Pedagogy: A Comprehensive Method of Jazz Education for Teacher and Student. Chicago: Maher Publications, 1979. Currently published by Alfred Publishing Company (Van Nuys, CA). Revised and enlarged edition forthcoming.

Jazz Styles and Analysis: Trombone. Chicago: Maher Publications, 1973. Currently published by Alfred Publishing Company (Van Nuys, CA).

Modern Concepts in Jazz Improvisation: A Comprehensive Method for All Musicians. A New Approach to Fourths, Pentatonics and Bitonals. Van Nuys, CA: Alfred Publishing Company, 1990.

Modern Jazz Duets for All Bass Clef Instruments. Volume 1: Cookin'. New York: Charles Colin, 1979.

Modern Jazz Duets for All Bass Clef Instruments. Volume 2: Smokin'. New York: Charles Colin, 1979.

Modern Jazz Duets for All Treble Clef Instruments. Volume 1: Cookin'. New York: Charles Colin, 1980.

Modern Jazz Duets for All Treble Clef Instruments. Volume 2: Smokin'. New York: Charles Colin, 1979.

A New Approach to Ear Training for the Jazz Musician. Lebanon, IN: Studio PR, 1976. Currently published by Columbia Pictures Publications/Belwin Mills (Miami, FL).

Techniques of Improvisation. Volume 1: A Method for Developing Improvisational Technique (Based on the Lydian Chromatic Concept by George Russell). Revised edition. Chicago: Maher Publications, 1971. Currently published by Alfred Publishing Company (Van Nuys, CA).

Techniques of Improvisation. Volume 2: The II V7 Progression. Revised edition. Chicago: Maher Publications, 1971. Currently published by Alfred Publishing Company (Van Nuys, CA).

      Techniques of Improvisation. Volume 3: Turnbacks. Chicago: Maher Publications, 1971. Currently published by Alfred Publishing Company (Van Nuys, CA).

      Techniques of Improvisation. Volume 4: Cycles. Chicago: Maher Publications, 1971. Currently published by Alfred Publishing Company (Van Nuys, CA).

Baker, David N. and Coker, Patty. Vocal Improvisation: An Instrumental Approach. Lebanon, IN: Studio PR, 1981. Currently published by Columbia Pictures Publications/Belwin Mills (Miami, FL).